My Notes

All I want to do is stay in my Sweater and watch Hallmark Holiday Movies & Pet My Cat all Day long

My Notes

My Notes

All I want to do is stay in my Sweater and watch Hallmark Holiday Movies & Pet My Cat all Day long

My Notes

My Notes

All I want to do is stay in my Sweater and watch Hallmark Holiday Movies & Pet My Cat all Day long

My Notes

My Notes

All I want to do is
stay in my Sweater
and watch Hallmark
Holiday Movies &
Pet My Cat all
Day long

My Notes

My Notes

All I want to do is stay in my Sweater and watch Hallmark Holiday Movies & Pet My Cat all Day long

My Notes

My Notes

All I want to do is stay in my Sweater and watch Hallmark Holiday Movies & Pet My Cat all Day long

My Notes

My Notes

All I want to do is stay in my Sweater and watch Hallmark Holiday Movies & Pet My Cat all Day long

My Notes

My Notes

All I want to do is stay in my sweater and watch Hallmark Holiday Movies & Pet My Cat all Day long

My Notes

My Notes

All I want to do is stay in my Sweater and watch Hallmark Holiday Movies & Pet My Cat all Day long

My Notes

My Notes

All I want to do is stay in my Sweater and watch Hallmark Holiday Movies & Pet My Cat all Day long

My Notes

My Notes

All I want to do is stay in my Sweater and watch Hallmark Holiday Movies & Pet My Cat all Day long

My Notes

My Notes

All I want to do is stay in my Sweater and watch Hallmark Holiday Movies & Pet My Cat all Day long

My Notes

My Notes

All I want to do is stay in my Sweater and watch Hallmark Holiday Movies & Pet My Cat all Day long

My Notes

My Notes

All I want to do is
stay in my Sweater
and watch Hallmark
Holiday Movies &
Pet My Cat all
Day long

My Notes

My Notes

All I want to do is stay in my Sweater and watch Hallmark Holiday Movies & Pet My Cat all Day long

My Notes

My Notes

All I want to do is stay in my Sweater and watch Hallmark Holiday Movies & Pet My Cat all Day long

My Notes

My Notes

All I want to do is stay in my Sweater and watch Hallmark Holiday Movies & Pet My Cat all Day long

My Notes

My Notes

All I want to do is stay in my Sweater and watch Hallmark Holiday Movies & Pet My Cat all Day long

My Notes

My Notes

All I want to do is
stay in my Sweater
and watch Hallmark
Holiday Movies &
Pet My Cat all
Day long

My Notes

My Notes

All I want to do is stay in my Sweater and watch Hallmark Holiday Movies & Pet My Cat all Day long

My Notes

My Notes

All I want to do is stay in my Sweater and watch Hallmark Holiday Movies & Pet My Cat all Day long

My Notes

My Notes

All I want to do is
stay in my Sweater
and watch Hallmark
Holiday Movies &
Pet My Cat all
Day long

My Notes

My Notes

All I want to do is stay in my sweater and watch Hallmark Holiday Movies & Pet My Cat all Day long

My Notes

My Notes

All I want to do is
stay in my Sweater
and watch Hallmark
Holiday Movies &
Pet My Cat all
Day long

My Notes

My Notes

All I want to do is stay in my Sweater and watch Hallmark Holiday Movies & Pet My Cat all Day long

My Notes

My Notes

All I want to do is
stay in my Sweater
and watch Hallmark
Holiday Movies &
Pet My Cat all
Day long

My Notes

My Notes

All I want to do is stay in my Sweater and watch Hallmark Holiday Movies & Pet My Cat all Day long

My Notes

My Notes

All I want to do is stay in my Sweater and watch Hallmark Holiday Movies & Pet My Cat all Day long

My Notes

My Notes

All I want to do is stay in my sweater and watch Hallmark Holiday Movies & Pet My Cat all Day long

My Notes

My Notes

All I want to do is stay in my Sweater and watch Hallmark Holiday Movies & Pet My Cat all Day long

My Notes

My Notes

All I want to do is stay in my Sweater and watch Hallmark Holiday Movies & Pet My Cat all Day long

My Notes

My Notes

All I want to do is stay in my Sweater and watch Hallmark Holiday Movies & Pet My Cat all Day long

My Notes

My Notes

All I want to do is stay in my Sweater and watch Hallmark Holiday Movies & Pet My Cat all Day long

My Notes

My Notes

All I want to do is stay in my Sweater and watch Hallmark Holiday Movies & Pet My Cat all Day long

My Notes

My Notes

All I want to do is
stay in my Sweater
and watch Hallmark
Holiday Movies &
Pet My Cat all
Day long

My Notes

My Notes

All I want to do is stay in my Sweater and watch Hallmark Holiday Movies & Pet My Cat all Day long

My Notes

My Notes

All I want to do is stay in my Sweater and watch Hallmark Holiday Movies & Pet My Cat all Day long

My Notes

My Notes

All I want to do is stay in my Sweater and watch Hallmark Holiday Movies & Pet My Cat all Day long

My Notes

My Notes

All I want to do is stay in my Sweater and watch Hallmark Holiday Movies & Pet My Cat all Day long

My Notes

My Notes

All I want to do is stay in my Sweater and watch Hallmark Holiday Movies & Pet My Cat all Day long

My Notes

My Notes

All I want to do is
stay in my Sweater
and watch Hallmark
Holiday Movies &
Pet My Cat all
Day long

My Notes

My Notes

All I want to do is stay in my Sweater and watch Hallmark Holiday Movies & Pet My Cat all Day long

My Notes

My Notes

All I want to do is stay in my Sweater and watch Hallmark Holiday Movies & Pet My Cat all Day long

My Notes

My Notes

All I want to do is stay in my Sweater and watch Hallmark Holiday Movies & Pet My Cat all Day long

My Notes

My Notes

All I want to do is stay in my Sweater and watch Hallmark Holiday Movies & Pet My Cat all Day long

My Notes

My Notes

All I want to do is stay in my Sweater and watch Hallmark Holiday Movies & Pet My Cat all Day long

My Notes

My Notes

All I want to do is stay in my Sweater and watch Hallmark Holiday Movies & Pet My Cat all Day long

My Notes

My Notes

All I want to do is
stay in my Sweater
and watch Hallmark
Holiday Movies &
Pet My Cat all
Day long

My Notes

My Notes

All I want to do is
stay in my Sweater
and watch Hallmark
Holiday Movies &
Pet My Cat all
Day long

My Notes

My Notes

All I want to do is stay in my Sweater and watch Hallmark Holiday Movies & Pet My Cat all Day long

My Notes

My Notes

All I want to do is stay in my Sweater and watch Hallmark Holiday Movies & Pet My Cat all Day long

My Notes

My Notes

All I want to do is
stay in my Sweater
and watch Hallmark
Holiday Movies &
Pet My Cat all
Day long

My Notes

My Notes

All I want to do is stay in my Sweater and watch Hallmark Holiday Movies & Pet My Cat all Day long

My Notes

My Notes

All I want to do is stay in my sweater and watch Hallmark Holiday Movies & Pet My Cat all Day long

My Notes

My Notes

All I want to do is stay in my Sweater and watch Hallmark Holiday Movies & Pet My Cat all Day long

My Notes

My Notes

All I want to do is
stay in my Sweater
and watch Hallmark
Holiday Movies &
Pet My Cat all
Day long

My Notes

My Notes

All I want to do is stay in my Sweater and watch Hallmark Holiday Movies & Pet My Cat all Day long

My Notes

My Notes

All I want to do is stay in my Sweater and watch Hallmark Holiday Movies & Pet My Cat all Day long

My Notes

My Notes

All I want to do is stay in my Sweater and watch Hallmark Holiday Movies & Pet My Cat all Day long

My Notes

My Notes

All I want to do is stay in my Sweater and watch Hallmark Holiday Movies & Pet My Cat all Day long

My Notes

CPSIA information can be obtained
at www.ICGtesting.com
Printed in the USA
LVHW060807281020
669935LV00015B/559